This book may be kept

FOURTEEN DAYS

A fine will be charged for each day the book is kept overtime.

JAN. 2 1 1993		
FEB. 1 5 1993		
NOV - 3 1995		
NOV 1 4 1996		
3-12-98		
NOV 3 0 1998		
	Crossroads College	
G.H. Cachiaras Memorial Library		
920 Mayowood Road SW, Rochester MN 55902		
507-535-3331		
GAYLORD 142		PRINTED IN U.S.A.

ng

on

ce

Don't
nt To

hall

.835
3697
9833

BAKER BOOK HOUSE
Grand Rapids, Michigan 49516

Copyright 1988 by
Baker Book House Company

ISBN: 0-8010-6228-4

Second printing, November 1988

Printed in the United States of America

This book is dedicated,
in loving memory,
to my mother
Melba.

She survived polio in her early years
when polio claimed lives.

She survived divorce in days
when it stigmatized her faith.

She single-parented three daughters
when women didn't work.

Much of what I have learned about survival
came from her.

Much of what I believe about hope
in the midst of heartache
she lived.

Contents

PART TWO You Can Survive

PART THREE Your Hope for Wholeness

Introduction

This is the book I was never going to write—not even for me. And if, perchance, I wrote it, I was *never* going to publish it or let you read it.

My divorce came on the heels of burying my baby, mother-in-law, and grandfather—and was followed shortly by the death of my stepfather; a major move; the loss of my home; and my struggle to gain financial independence in an economy blessed with teachers looking for work.

Divorce was excruciating pain; it was something that happened to others, not to Christian couples who were active in church work. Yet it did. Justin, our second son, was born a "special child," and during his short life of four and a half months on this earth, God was our strength and guide. But then Justin died, and his father, an alcoholic, turned again to the bottle. Our almost ten-year marriage became a statistic— one of the millions that end in divorce. My three-year-old son, Jeff, and I were left to create a home out of life's shambles.

Caring, well-meaning people would say, "God is going to use this to help others!"

And I would respond sincerely, sarcastically, and bitterly, "That's wonderful! I've prayed all my life that I could be a bad example."

For those of you who still struggle with this bitterness, let me assure you that there is hope! It has taken hard work; it has taken much time; it has taken my willingness to look honestly at me and to make some changes in my life. But God has healed me! I now am deeply gratified that God would choose to use me—and my experience—to help another. I couldn't do that in my own power, but God is in the business of mending broken hearts and affirming his children as they minister to one another.

This book began on one of those nights when I talked too much. Perhaps in an effort to quiet me, my Aunt Pansy handed me an empty book. The first draft is her original, punctuated by my tears. Telling me to write what I had been saying (non-stop), she commented, "You never know when one of my children will need to hear what you have to say."

A panic welled within. Until that time I was so engrossed in my own loss that I honestly didn't realize someone else could hurt as I did. But something better than the birth of a book happened as a result of her words. They also brought the beginning of God's message to me: sorrow, placed in his hands, is not wasted.

I must confess that this message was wrought

through my tears—and through my prayers—and in my lonely hours. And I must confess that, healing behind me, it was painful to go back and relive the hurt that so nearly destroyed me when I lived it the first time. It will be worth it, though, if this message can bring hope to you.

Surviving Separation and Divorce is divided into three parts. Part 1 describes the physical, emotional, and spiritual reactions common to divorce. It is not a pretty account—but divorce is not a thing of beauty. I wrote it because I felt so alone when I faced it, and I thought I was losing my mind, along with my marriage. I have learned that these reactions are common; I share them to let you know they are normal.

Part 2 gives you keys for survival—strategies for holding on when holding on is all you can do. It provides both spiritual and practical guidance. The spiritual guidance is there to remind you not to give up hope on the One who can free you. The practical guidance is given to help you make it through the long and lonely nights until you decide again that life is worth living.

Part 3 is your hope for wholeness—your growth, beyond survival. You see, God doesn't want you just to survive. He wants you to have life victorious. Section 3 will describe areas of potential growth and some danger signs on your road to wholeness.

May God use this to help you survive until, someday, you can radiantly and confidently help another. He will not give you the hope he gave me. Instead he will use my experience and that of many others to give you a hope all your own.

PART 1

Divorce— The Life-style

Divorce

What an ugly word! Synonymous to failure, sin, death, hell.

You're new to the world of divorce? Welcome.

Your body will go through the motions of living, but your spirit and your soul will reside in hell. They'll stay there for a long, long time—an eternity. Each day will last forever, and the promise of tomorrow looms an omen over your head.

Reflection

> The sun will rise tomorrow . . .
>   (but you've forgotten why).
> You'll awaken in the morning . . .
>   (and maybe wonder how to die).

1

Mind: Closed for Repairs

You'll be driving down the street and forget where you're going and where you've been.

You'll start to do some old, familiar chore only to discover you can't remember how.

You'll make a favorite recipe and forget one of the major ingredients.

You'll call a friend and forget why.

You'll go after something at least a dozen times but forget what you wanted when you get there.

Your eyes will read words, but your mind has forgotten how to blend them together to make meaning.

Reflection

Sound like you? Welcome. You're in the land called "Mourning."

But move along! Somewhere down the road there *is* an exit. Your task is to find it—but you can't get out by going back.

2

Oh, Fatigue!

Y ou work hard, hard, hard doing meaningless chores. If you slowed down, you would have to think. If you allowed yourself to think, you would have to cry. You can't handle another day of futile tears, so you work even though you're exhausted—and even though you work hard, you accomplish nothing.

It seems you're always sighing, aching, yawning; and you flit from one task to another. You *never* feel good, and you're always tired.

Hours before your usual bedtime, you fall into bed exhausted. Then you awaken at bedtime, unable to sleep and plagued with thoughts . . . feelings . . . fears . . . tears.

You lie awake all night and want to sleep all day.

Reflection

In the eyes of my mind,
  I was plagued 'oft to see
An old, broken lady—
  It seemed wrong, her to be.

Her shoulders were laden
  And frantic with sorrow.
She moved with great effort,
  As fearing tomorrow.

She sighed, and she flitted.
  Each step cost a mile;
And she couldn't be still
  Though she yawned all the while.

I glared with disgust, and
  I chose not to see.
But in flashback the eyes
  Caught my own. It was me.

3

Sleeplessness

When you are awakened by a nightmare, your mind can no longer control your thoughts. With the dawn of reality comes a dark cloud called despair.

You scream . . .

You cry . . .

You pray . . .

You toss . . .

But you don't feel any better.

You stare at the blackness, unable to sleep and afraid to get up.

You try all the tricks—counting sheep, breathing deeply, praying, imaging, drinking warm milk.

Nothing works. You lie awake, abandoned, afraid.

Reflection

No one ever told me that grief felt so like fear. I am not afraid, but the sensation is like being afraid. The same fluttering in the stomach, the same rest-lessness, the yawning. I keep on swallowing.

At other times it feels like being mildly drunk, or concussed. There is a sort of invisible blanket be-tween the world and me. I find it hard to take in what anyone says. . . .

C. S. LEWIS

A Grief Observed (Harper & Row, 1963)
Used by permission.

4

Phantom Fears

In the middle of the night, you awake with a start to hear someone walking down your hallway. You lie frozen in your fear. As the footsteps near you, you cease to breathe—but your heart pounds so loudly that it gives you away. Each footstep echoes in your ears, and you reach a state of panic trying to decide whether to run or scream.

You actually feel the bed move and strain in the darkness to see someone standing beside you. You hear deep breathing, see the shadow of a face hovering over you, and feel the movement of bated breath stirring the stillness around you.

But that someone never quite touches you—it just tortures you with fear. Finally you scream and reach for the light—only to find yourself alone.

The footsteps must have been inside you.

Reflection

God hath not given us a spirit of fear, but of power (2 Tim. 1:7).

Lord, those two spirits are battling for me right now—first one ruling, then the other.

I belong to you so the spirit of power is going to win. I just wish it would hurry.

(. . . and I wish I could convince myself of it.)

5

Those Dreams and Nightmares!

In the middle of the night, your love returns. As you sleep, you sense him undress—as he has so many times before—and slip into bed beside you.

You feel him hold you in his arms, and for a moment everything is as it has always been. You are content; you are comforted; you are complete.

You feel his hands caress your body, and you hear him speak tender words of love. At first your body is a mixture of feelings—you long for his words to be true, but something faint in your memory recalls a hurt. You struggle to forget the pain and begin to enjoy his touch—but just as your body begins to respond to his loving embrace, you awaken . . . alone . . . and cry.

You cry because you miss him.

You cry because you need him.

You cry because it felt so good to be held again, even if it was only a dream.

You cry because you are afraid.

You feel a strange mixture of longing, rage, love, hate, frustration, and desire.

Finally, you can cry no more. You fall into an exhausted, restless sleep.

In just moments, the alarm goes off, finding you depleted of energy and purpose, feeling completely unable to face another day. Yet you go through the motions, and those who watch think you're getting back to normal. You're not. But they don't understand, so you pretend, and the emptiness stays locked inside you.

Reflection

It's so hard to live at the level of "what is" rather than "what might have been."

When is memory destructive?
  When you refuse to move ahead?

When is memory constructive?
  When it challenges us, even though we hurt?
  When we remember, but are free to love again?

Will I ever be free?

6

Glorious, Nauseous Food!

Y̱ou awaken with a gnawing, oppressive hunger, and you cook a big breakfast. But after only two bites, you find yourself sick to your stomach, and you can't eat. You get a warped satisfaction from watching the garbage disposal devour your food.

Then you get the hunger-shakes and stuff yourself with junk.

By lunchtime, you are sickishly full and too nauseous to eat a balanced meal.

There is no in-between. You're either nauseous or shaking from hunger, so you snack all day long.

If you need to gain weight, you lose weight on this diet. If you need to lose weight, you gain weight munching junk.

Either way, you have no energy. Your food doesn't seem to remember what it is supposed to do.

Reflection

Sometimes I have dessert—then dinner—then dessert again. And I come away nauseated only to have another candy bar.

Sometimes, when I don't have a child watching, I skip dinner and have half-a-pound (or more) of candy instead. When I have a child watching, I eat anyway and sneak the candy.

It isn't just that my body craves sweets. It's that awful taste in my mouth. It's always there.

And I need to eat something to appease the nervousness in my head.

7

Oh, Cursed Creativity

You wonder what he's doing, and you find a dozen reasons each day to drive by and look at his car.

You find a million creative excuses to call—a faucet needs fixing, the lawn needs mowing, the car makes a funny noise.

Somewhere inside yourself you remember how disgusted you were when friends acted this way, and you hate yourself for not being more independent. You despise the fact that you need him so desperately, but you swallow your pride a million times each day, just for the sick comfort you receive from a moment of being at his side.

But . . .

It hurts just as much to be with him, so calloused and aloof, as it does to be alone.

You wonder if this is really the same man you married. The man you are trying to regain seems so like a stranger.

But, then, most of the time now, you're also a stranger to yourself.

Reflection

There are times when I *hate* you—like the time I had to rush our Jeff to emergency—alone.

You were the strong one! You were always there. You gave me faith and strength and courage. With you beside me, I knew it would be all right.

Today I didn't have you—and I hurt—and I hated. I didn't know—without you—if it *would* be all right. I wondered why someone so tender as you would create a life and then desert it.

But my hate didn't bring you back, and my love couldn't keep you from going.

We lived through the ordeal. Jeff is fine.

8

Escaping

You need to hide. You want something to ease the pain. You consider getting drunk—and you are shocked at yourself for even thinking about it.

You need to be loved. You feel like fair game for whatever man happens to be around. You lash out in anger when you realize that he taught you to enjoy your sexuality—then left you frustrated, trying to deal with it now, alone. You wonder if God really expects celibacy of the divorced. But your mind won't think through anything just now. It's not a good year for making decisions.

You would like to go to a party and get high; you would like to find someone to hold you in his arms. But . . . you can't afford a babysitter. And that, too, brings tears of rage and anger. He's free to roam, without a care—and you're stuck at home with the kids.

You make it through the night somehow—still frustrated—and wonder if it pays to be moral.

Or—maybe. . .

You go in spite of the kids and in spite of the money. You do get high. You end up with an amorous admirer—but you're still frustrated and discontent. And you still have that awful, gnawing, empty feeling inside.

And now you have another kind of guilt to cope with. And you feel strangely bound to another—one you know only through the shackles of your wounded imagination.

Reflection

Sometimes it's almost unbearable. Sometimes I just wish I had a man—any man.

Sometimes I wish I could be married again to *anyone*, just long enough to make love. Even for just one night. Sometimes, in fact, I'd settle for an evening.

Why is it that some people pray, and God miraculously delivers them or sends what they ask for? But when *I* pray, I just keep plugging along and eventually people say I'm doing better. But I'm not. They just don't look very closely.

Life wasn't meant to be lived this way.

9

Reaching Out

You call your friends. In your depression, you don't know what to say. You speak in two- or three-word sentences followed by strained periods of silence. You feel you made a fool of yourself again.

Next time you don't call—you sit, withdrawn, alone, in darkness—wishing they'd call you—but they don't.

Sometimes they do, but it's never while you're sitting and wishing and lonely.

Reflection

It hurts. I'm one, and things are done in twos.

It's a holiday, and I'm home alone. They're probably all getting together. They probably think I'm out somewhere—or they don't think of me at all.

I'm only one, and they're all two.

Oh, God, how I hate being "one of the singles."

Jesus, did you hate being single sometimes, too?

10

Illness

Every time your friends invite you to do something fun with them, you or the kids get sick, and you have to cancel.

The first time a man asks you out, you can't go because you've developed a migraine headache.

You finally go out, after hours of psyching yourself up to have fun. You do—and you are pleasantly surprised and quite pleased with yourself. Then on the road home, you begin to claw at yourself and discover you have developed a severe case of the hives.

It seems the only time you're well enough to do something fun is when your kids are sick and you have to stay home with them.

It's a strange, depressing, and lonely existence. Probably even God doesn't care.

Reflection

What I dislike most about being single is that I rarely feel feminine.

I earn the living and have become a respected member of the business world—but I'd just like to be a woman! I'd like to entertain again—and cook—and wear sexy clothes—and have someone protect me.

Instead I attend meetings, eat in restaurants, wear business suits, and protect a little boy—alone.

I don't feel masculine.

I don't feel feminine.

Does that make me a neuter? Yuk!

There is hope . . . you *will* feel better about yourself. It just takes time!

11

Help for the Children

You watch your children. You notice subtle personality changes. The quiet one is loud and obnoxious now, and the outgoing one has become clingy. They have nightmares; and they, too, don't eat the way they used to. You wonder if you have destroyed them.

Sometimes you launch out at them in a rage. The rage is inside you, but the children are there to receive your angry and misdirected tears.

Sometimes you cry as you stand over their sleeping forms at night. You ask them to forgive you. You ask God to forgive you for the kind of a parent you have been. You vow you'll do better. For their sake, you promise to pull your life together.

But you launch out again. The rage inside you will not be controlled by guilt or by reason. In fact, right now it refuses even to be controlled by God.

The children keep you going through the motions of living. You value them more than you do your own

life, but they compound the tremendous cloud of guilt
and despair that envelops you.

Reflection

A song keeps ringing in my ears. . .
    "In those precious lonely hours
        Jesus let me know that I was his own."
It's been so long, God, since I've felt your presence.
It's been so long since I've felt a part of a cause.
It's been so long since I've felt your power
    surpassing my weakness.
I've been living in life's gullies for so long
    I can hardly remember a mountaintop
And I don't think I'll ever see one again.

12

Supplying Your Needs

You don't have any money. You could live without food. In fact, you would like to starve yourself to death. That would show him!

But you have children to care for.

You swallow your pride—if you have any left—and you go to the welfare office to ask about food stamps. You're humiliated, but your children are hungry.

You look quickly around the office, hoping no one recognizes you. You hide in a corner. You must wait for hours, and you start to leave at least a dozen times, each time realizing that you have no way to provide for your children if you do. When they finally call your name, you run quickly to the door, hoping no one heard and no one knows you.

It takes all the self-control you can muster to live through the interview. You hate him for putting you through this. You hate yourself. You hate the welfare worker. Somewhere, deep inside, you wonder if you even hate God.

You work hard to control yourself in the office, but you cannot contain your emotions once you walk out the door. You sob uncontrollably in your car; and it's a long, stormy while before you're able to drive home.

It never gets any better with the welfare office. They seem to work overtime to humiliate you.

The food stamps finally arrive, and you switch markets because you're embarrassed to shop where people know you.

Switching markets doesn't help; the humiliation lives within.

Will life ever have any joy again? Yes! Give yourself more time!

Reflection

Dear God,

I just read a book. The author said she didn't want to leave her children to return to work after her husband died so she prayed about it—and you opened up a door for her to work in her home. She could be gainfully employed *and* be a full-time mother.

Do you remember how I prayed? And doors didn't open, and he had to go to nursery school, and I switched him so many, many times because I didn't feel good about any of them? And I felt so guilty leaving him, but I had no other choice—it was that or starve.

Were you with me then, God? I asked you to be.

And I read another book. The author told about how you found for her just the right apartment—immediately after she remembered to ask you.

Do you remember that I prayed, too, when I had to move? And I found rudeness and humiliation and *No Children* signs and landlords that didn't rent to "your kind."

Do you remember that I prayed before I faced the realtor who made crude, suggestive remarks? The apartment that left me crawling with fleas and flea bites? The neighborhood that left me afraid even to get out of the car?

And do you remember, God, that even though I prayed about it, when I finally found a place, it wasn't available for two months, and I had to impose on relatives again? And the only place available to me was just next door to painful memories?

Were you with me then, God? I asked you to be. Help me to feel your presence more keenly.

13

Life Goes On

Life goes on like this for days . . . weeks . . . months . . . maybe even years. It doesn't get any better for a long, long time. But eventually it *does* get better.

Faith is a thing of the past. You have none—not even a mustard-seed's size.

Reflection

I'm writing to keep from crying.
I'll cry when I finish writing.

Summing Up

Welcome.

If this describes you, you've just entered the miserable existence of divorce.

> I sure hope there's a heaven.
> I've already been to hell.

Reflection

> . . . Maybe I ought to say
> I'm on top of it
> praise the Lord
> things are great
> but they're not.
> Tonight
> it's all
> gray slush.

JOSEPH BAYLY

"A Psalm in a hotel room"
Psalms of My Life (Tyndale, 1969)

37

PART 2

You Can Survive

It feels so awful! How can I ever survive?
I don't really know if I want to.

Yes, you can survive. It will take time, and it will be hard work.

There are some things you need to remember. They are facts, regardless of how you feel.

There are some things you need to do. They won't be easy, but they are necessary to your wholeness.

There are some things you need to avoid. That, too, will be difficult. And the fact of the difficulty may surprise—or even devastate—you.

Pray, as you read this section on how to survive, that God will speak to you through it. What he says to you is far more important than anything I could say, for he knows your situation, yes, even better than you do. He loves you, even more than you love yourself. And he loves your lost love with a love that far surpasses your longings. My words may or may not be true in your situation. His words are always true; they are always spoken in love; and they always bring you the option of receiving power to respond.

Reflection

Christian psychologist and speaker Dr. Frank Freed said he learned in seminary that God has glorious power to bring us through our every circumstance in life—not just "somehow," but "triumphantly."

As he went on to recount his experience in the foxholes during the war, he tapped a prosthesis where once an arm had been. He concluded that there were times in his life when he would be deeply grateful if God could just get him through—"somehow."

As you move through your experience of divorce survival, it is okay if most days you just make it through *somehow*. But you will discover, at the other end of your sorrow, that your faithfulness in life's somehows allows God to lead you into life *triumphant*. Although your vision is dimmed now because of your circumstances, he is still the God who does "exceeding abundantly above all that we ask or think" (Eph. 3:20).

14

God's Love Is

Never ever forget that God loves you. You may not feel it. You may not see signs of his love in your life. You may not feel worthwhile or lovable—*but you are loved*. You can rest in that knowledge. God's love *is;* it never changes. It doesn't depend on you or on your circumstances.

Reflection

God's love is not a feeling; it's a fact.
Most of my life I've wished it was a feeling.

15

You Are "Okay"—For Now

Remember that what you are experiencing is normal. You're in shock; you're going through a universal grief process. It is "okay" for you to be this way—for now. It won't *really* last forever.

You feel that no one else has ever hurt as you do, and you are quite sure that no other living soul can understand. You feel as though you are losing your mind, too—in fact, you are quite sure that you *are* going crazy.

This is normal. This is grief. "This, too, shall pass." It takes an average of two years to recover, but this *really* miserable stage won't last that long.

Hang on!

Reflection

The early days—

I know there's a light at the end of the tunnel, but I don't have enough faith to believe I'll ever get to it. I can't see it or feel it, and I don't have the strength to go on.

Later—

Suddenly I'm not mad at God any more. I'm not mad at anyone, really. I'm just numb.

I don't know which was worse.

And finally—

The midnight is finally over, and my soul can see the sunrise! It feels so good to have a song in my heart. I thought it had gone forever.

16

Search Your Soul

Search your soul for hidden sins.

> If God convicts, confess.
> > Accept God's promise of forgiveness, and
> > Forgive yourself.

> If God brings no sin to light,
> > Don't torture yourself looking for faults.
> > Move on.

Remember that God's message is clear and that God affirms. If the message you are hearing does not affirm and uplift you as a person, it is not from God, the author of goodness. God clearly denounces sin, but he doesn't destroy people who seek him.

A friend once told me that if the message was confusing, it wasn't from God. As I walked—or crawled—through my divorce, most of what I heard, sensed, and felt confused me. If her words are true—and I think they are—the self-condemnation and self-destruction I heard came from another power—one who would be delighted to defeat me! The confusion in my mind that demanded action was not from God. I must wait for action until confusion becomes vision.

We need not—in fact, we ought not—carry the load of guilt confessed.

Reflection

If we confess our sin, he is faithful and just to forgive our sin and to cleanse us from all unrighteousness.

1 John 1:9

This is fact, not opinion. It's based on God's Word, not on your feelings. We have no right to hold a grudge against one whom God has forgiven. If you have confessed and asked forgiveness, God has forgiven you and you are free to forgive yourself.

Whether we can see his handiwork clearly or not, God's promises are true; and God—the God of integrity—*always* keeps his promises!

SHARON MARSHALL

Justin, Heaven's Baby (Beacon Hill, 1983)

17

Abolish "If Only"

Learn to distinguish between destructive feelings and guilt. The "if onlys" are damning and destructive. When you get a case of the "If only I hads," cast it off quickly!

Nothing can change your yesterday, but yesterday can destroy your today and rob you of tomorrow.

Reflection

Sometimes I dream about
    What it would be like to have
A big family. (Or is it really
    Two little boys and a husband?
Normal fun, quiet times, and noise
    That are never more to be?)

I thought I had quit asking why,
    But sometimes when I'm lonely
It just pops up again.

Why did *my* husband stray?
Why did *my* baby die?
Why me?

Please, God, protect my little Jeff from harm!

18

Face Loneliness—Alone!

Learn to distinguish between loneliness and guilt. Most of what you feel is loneliness. Confess it to Christ as a deep-soul need, not as a sin. God does not condemn us for needing the person and presence of another.

Don't seek to fill your aloneness through having an affair or through a quick remarriage. That postpones the time you will need to heal, adds another emotional scar to your already-hurting heart, and involves another person, compounding your grief.

If you fall into sin, confess it and allow Christ to forgive you. Don't fall into the common traps of rationalization and self-hate. Dishonesty—even with yourself—prevents Christ's healing, and healing must occur before he can give you a lasting recovery. Self-condemnation is Satan's tool to render you ineffective. If you sin, God has given you the gift of confession. As did the prodigal's father, he accepts you back as sons (or daughters), not as servants.

And, yes, he *will* give you a lasting recovery if you will give him both time and permission.

Reflection

> I'm a misfit, God.
>   I don't belong
> With the "happy hour"
>   Crowd . . .
> Musical beds . . .
>   Surface friends.
>
> But I'm lonely, Lord,
>   And I've only begun.
>
> Will I survive this?
>   I don't know.
> Right now I'm not sure I will—
>   Even with your help.

19

Be Honest With God

God knows what you're like;
God knows how you feel;
God knows what you're thinking.

When you think you're fooling God, you're only fooling yourself . . . so . . . *be honest with God.*

God can deal only with what you give him. He can handle your:

Anger . . .
Wrath . . .
Disbelief . . .
Rage . . .
Lust . . .
Hate . . .
Wrong Behavior . . .

Confess it.

God can handle your:

Depression . . .
Poor self-image . . .

Lack of confidence . . .

Frustration . . .

Talk to him about it. Place it in his hands.

Come to think of it, is there anything God can't deal with? Yes! Your lies. Until you are honest with him (and with yourself), he must wait.

When you hand God your battered, broken spirit, your angry heart, your aloneness, your guilt, he *can* and *will* send healing.

It's true. He's in the business of "working together for good."

It takes time. It usually takes longer than you want it to—not because God isn't willing or listening, but because it takes time to stop bleeding, heal, and grow. If your grief has been compounded by circumstances or other major losses, it will take much longer. Mine was compounded by multiple deaths in my immediate family. The combination of circumstances brought on by these multiple traumas took me several years to resolve. I didn't think I would live that long when I started. Now I feel like my life has just begun.

Unfortunately, here's more bad news. Grief is often compounded. You've heard it said, "Troubles come in bundles." You compound your grief by rebounding or by having an affair. It is compounded by a major move or a change in economic or employment status. It is compounded if you experience more than one major loss within a short period of time, such as divorce following the handicap or death of a child (which is too often the case).

Reflection

If we pray only our holy prayers—
    our unholy thoughts remain unholy still—
        and pace the cage, feeding on our fantasies
                    and daydreams.
            And sometimes—
                they grow strong enough
                to break out and wreak havoc!
Then a "holy" person can do an "unholy" thing
                    And we wonder:
                        How can that be?
It is because the "unacceptable" thoughts and
                        hungers and
                        desires and
                        yearnings
    were not truly opened up to God for his
                            renewing,
                            cleansing,
                            healing grace!
Whatever you desire, don't define it beforehand.
    Pour it all out to God, and his Spirit
        will define and edit and cleanse."

                        REUBEN WELCH

We Really Do Need To Listen (Impact)

20

Know God Understands

". . .there is no searching of his understanding" (Isa. 40:28). He knows how deeply you hurt. Consider this:

He was betrayed, too.

He was rejected, too.

Those he loved most turned him away, too; and on the cross he prayed a prayer for their forgiveness.

He, too, has loved as deeply as you—only to have that love rejected.

He understands, and he cares. He even understands when the intensity of your hurt makes you long for another more than you long for him—and he agonizes with you as he waits to be your comfort.

Reflection

> Missing your love
> with God's so
> close at hand.
>
> It seems somehow
> a sacrilege . . .
>
> but I think
> He understands.

> PETER MCWILLIAMS

> *How To Survive The Loss Of a Love*
> (Simon & Schuster)

He really does understand. With the comfort of that truth, you can move on.

21

Release the One You Love

Release the one you love to the God who loves him far more than you ever could!

It was a great morning when I awoke to discover that God loved my love far more than I did; that God was far wiser than I in how to lead him back; that God could go wherever he was, but I couldn't any longer handle the wondering and worrying about him; that *I could trust the one I love into the hands of the God who loves us both.*

I could bear the burden no longer, so I released him into the hands of the almighty, loving, powerful God—the God who created him in the first place.

No, God didn't bring him back to me. But neither did I, in spite of all my efforts. What God did, though, when I allowed it, was to release me from the heavy load of hurt that robbed me daily of my life.

I think there were tears in heaven when our home was broken. There were tears of compassion for my hurt, and there were sobs of sorrow for my love who had chosen to turn away from God. I believe the heavens mourned for each of us, and God's love reached out to us both. Only God could love that completely.

Yield your loved one into the hands of God. Do pray for him—but remember that you are powerless to change him, and you *can* trust him to the God who gave his life to save him.

Reflection

> I'm getting better.
> I long for arms to hold me—
>   but not your arms.
> "Someone's" arms
>   Someday
>   When God sees fit.
>
> You'll go on to live in spite of me.
>   I'll go on to live only
>   When I let you go.
>
> I believe someday you'll make it;
>   But it took me a long, long time to know
>   That we wouldn't make it
>   together.

22

Give Yourself Time

If you knew me, you would realize how difficult it is for me to say this. You would never speak of me and patience in the same breath. You might even recall that familiar cliché that says "Practice what you preach!" And as much as I hate to be told, I must tell you to be *patient*. It takes time.

Nothing can replace that which you must experience if you want to be truly whole again (and you do—even if you don't think so now).

That hurt . . . that emptiness . . . that anger . . . that hatred . . . that frustration . . . that despair . . . that guilt . . . that loneliness . . . that rage . . . that self-hate—*all* that wages a battle on your inside—must come out before God can replace it with his goodness, and healing can become complete.

If you just let the surface heal over, what remains on the inside will fester and erupt periodically for the rest of your life. It will rob you of a future intimate relationship. It will surprise you in outbursts over minor offenses—outbursts that are out of character for you.

If you turn to sex, alcohol, drugs (even prescription drugs over an extended period of time, without proper counsel), you just postpone the process. Let that which wages a battle inside you be released as soon as you can, and in as creative a way as possible—but don't bury it, rush it, or deny it—unless you want to pay for it for the rest of your life.

It takes time.

It's painful.

It seems like you'll hurt forever.

You won't. Be patient.

Reflection

Your sun *will* shine again—brighter!
(. . . Whether you want it to or not).

23

Discharge the Rage

How do you get rid of this venom that would defeat you? That depends on you, your talents, and your personality.

You may need to destroy something—but don't destroy something you may later regret or something that is rightfully a part of your children's heritage (like your wedding pictures). Destroy something that is symbolic of a friction between the two of you rather than something that brings memories of vowed love.

I tore down, limb by limb, a bushy tree that was half dead. I had begged him to replace it for years, so it became my symbol of rage. As I chopped each limb, alone, I cried and prayed and told both him and God of my hurt, just as if they were standing there. And it didn't change the facts, but it kept me from doing something rash.

Replace what you destroy with something that brings you joy. I replaced the tree with flowers that I could pick for vases. Somehow that was symbolic of the fact that a new life was, indeed, possible, although at the time I didn't believe it.

And, because my loved one was an alcoholic, I broke every wine and alcohol bottle I could find. This helped to curb the almost uncontrollable urge I had to crash my car into the bar or to burn down the place that represented, in my mind, the destruction of my marriage. Sometimes it took every ounce of self-control I had to keep from doing this. Bottle-breaking escapades helped release some of the terror that was inside me, but I got so angry about having to clean up the mess that I don't recommend it. Chopping trees was better.

Playing "Why don't you . . . God!" helped me release the rage.

I'd yell, "Why don't *you* burn the bar down? They can't throw *you* in jail!"

He didn't, you know, but playing "Why don't you . . ." and "If I were you, God . . ." got me through a lot of tough times.

Perhaps a pattern of intimate conversations with God is necessary for this. I may doubt that he will do anything about my problems; I may doubt his willingness to help—but I need not doubt that he hears me and loves me and understands what I *mean* rather than what I say. When I don't even know what I mean, I know that God does.

Whatever works for you to help you physically discharge your frustration (sports, cleaning, decorating, and so forth), do it, but do it as you cry and pray—preferably out loud. This opens the door for God to cleanse you as you work.

Reflection

Satan couldn't defeat me through alcohol or sex or drugs or money or bitterness. Instead, he defeated one I loved and trusted. In doing so, he *almost* won two victories because he almost defeated me through the divorce. He doesn't need to worry about me while I'm licking my wounds and feeling sorry for myself. And he used God's laws to stab me with a knife of guilt.

God, forgive me for wallowing in defeat for so long. I'm ready to hold your hand and move on.

24

Worship in a New Way

You were created by a God who is worthy of praise. He created you in such a way that when you do not worship him, you feel a void within. Yet while you are hurting, you may not feel affirmed when you worship in traditional ways.

You may sit through a moving service and wonder why everyone else seems to feel something when you are numb. You may sit through a quiet, peaceful service, sobbing uncontrollably and feeling like you have robbed others of their right to worship. You may wonder why you sit through a service at all and feel like a hypocrite. You may read your Bible and wonder what it says and why you read it. You may pray and wonder why you bothered when your prayers don't get any higher than your ceiling. (In fact, some days prayers reaching as high as the ceiling could feel like a victory!)

In times like this, you worship through your sorrow, using the talent that God has given you. Writing helped me tremendously—it was my survival. I would write letters to God, sometimes sobbing uncontrollably as I expressed my hurt and disappointment. I would write letters to God, angry, expressing my disbelief. I would write letters to my loved one expressing my love, anger, or hate. I would write letters to my family, expressing my frustration that they didn't seem to understand. Of course, I never mailed these letters. In fact, sometimes I burned them over my sink as my "burning sacrifice" to God. But writing, for me, let me express what wouldn't come out in spoken words. It helped me to clarify what I was feeling and to sort out my thoughts. It helped me make it through many a sleepless, agonizing night. It helped put words to my tears—and by adding words, I felt released rather than frenzied when I finished.

And guess what I learned, years later, when I attended a Christian writers' conference! Writing is a form of worship. Hearing that released the load brought by years of buried guilt. How neat! I *was* worshiping during those dark days when I left most church services in tears, numb, and lonely. I would go home and write.

I needed to go through the motions of worship, and God rewards our faithfulness. Do remain faithful to your church. But when traditional worship leaves you feeling empty because of your hurting heart, worship God by giving him your sorrow in your own special way.

What is your creative talent? Writing? Crafts? Painting? Teaching? Coaching? Singing? Cooking?

Do it! Do lots of it! Do it to the glory of God. Make it your special way of saying:

> God, I hurt; but I love you.
> I can't feel you, but I'll trust you.
> I can't remember why, but I'll serve you.
> I'm angry and confused, but you're all I have.
> I'll be true—even if I have to wait until I get to heaven to feel good again.

Yes, you can worship by giving your sorrow to Jesus! He can replace it with joy only when it is in his hands.

Reflection

> You can paint your sorrow on a canvas;
>   You can sing your sorrow in a song.
> You can write your sorrow in a letter . . .
>   Then give your sorrow to the Lord.

25

Honor Your Convictions

Remain true to your convictions, even when it hurts.

Becoming single again places you in a world with a different lifestyle and moral code than the one you know. Don't give up your values. That adds confusion to your life and lowers your already-wounded self-esteem. Talk to God about how to survive in this new world, but remain true to yourself.

Sunday is the pits! Worship in body even when you can't worship in spirit. We always attended church together. It hurt to go alone. Sometimes I left in tears, but I went because I knew I should. It was a way of holding on to something I knew to be stable during a time when I was not. Perhaps I went to church because I was afraid of having to spend a Sunday morning at home alone. Sometimes my son, Jeff, was the *only* reason I attended—but Jeff is reason supreme. Whatever your reason, be faithful. Don't worry about feeling hypocritical because you can't participate emotionally as you have in the past—and don't worry about what others will think. You are responsible only for yourself and answerable only to God. He knows your heart and will honor the soul that seeks him in practice until it can again seek him in spirit.

Reflection

The secret is this: To really "live," that is to find life reasonably satisfying, you must have an adequate and realistic self-image that you can live with. You must find your self acceptable to "you." You must have a wholesome self-esteem. You must have a self that you can trust and believe in. You must have a self that you are not ashamed to "be," and one that you can feel free to express creatively, rather than to hide or cover up.

MAXWELL MALTZ

Psycho-Cybernetics (Wilshire, 1983)

26

Reach Out

Find someone to whom you can give yourself—not sexually, but in love. I was a teacher so I invested my surplus of love in need of an object in my students—and my teaching will never be the same! I'm not sure they noticed a difference in me but I noticed a difference in myself.

God created us with a need to give ourselves in love. When we no longer have a spouse to whom we can give, we are in danger of "smother-loving" our children or of a destructive relationship. As you actively invest yourself in others, you will be contributing toward your own wholeness.

We taught the church teens, and it hurt to see them when I felt I was such a failure as their role model. Even though I went home for a bout with tears, confusion, and guilt after talking to them, I was stronger for having faced the situation. Years later, I taught the teens again—alone. It took a long time before I could handle it emotionally, for teens were a cher-

ished memory of our "together" projects. Teaching
the church teens alone helped to heal my heart. I
learned that all God needed was my willingness for
him to use me effectively—anytime, in any way he
chooses—regardless of my preconceived ideas about
how things "should" be done.

What is your area of service? Continue to do it,
even though you don't feel like it. You will find that
God created us with a need to give of ourselves. In
investing your life in another, in service to God, you
will be contributing to your recovery.

Who are your special people? Babies? Toddlers?
Young children? Teens? Women? The elderly? The
handicapped? Find a way to serve and love them.

Reflection

> . . . for it is in giving
> that we receive . . .

27

Seek Professional Help

You need the listening ear of a trained professional who is also trained in the Bible. Your friends will understand how you hurt for a week or two—maybe even a month or two—but *not* for a year or two! It took much longer for me because so many losses were piled together.

Two years seemed like an eternity to be hurting when I started my grief process. I thought I would never quit hurting, but I couldn't imagine giving up two years of my life to grieving. In reality, I gave up much more of my life than that! Perhaps a trained professional could have shortened that time if I had been willing to invest more time in counseling.

I thought a counselor couldn't change things so wouldn't be of help to me. And a counselor couldn't repair my marriage, bring back my baby, pay my bills, or find me a job. But he could—and did—provide a much-needed outlet for my tears so I didn't have to burden my friends anymore—and so I could make it through my day at work without going to pieces (most of the time). He could help me to understand and cope with the behaviors of my son, who was also mourning our losses; and he could help to repair my own shattered self-esteem.

Seek help first from your minister. Ask your minister for a referral to a professional. Most churches with counseling centers and Christian counseling clinics have provision for low-income people to receive help. Most insurance policies will pay at least a portion of your charges.

If the first counselor doesn't help you or doesn't seem to be right, seek another. You deserve to be whole! And you can be whole again.

Reflection

I went to his office only because I had promised her I would go. The words had trouble finding their way out of my mouth. Finally, I "dumped" my problems and arose to leave, saying, "But there's nothing you can do about it. Thank you for your time."

He stopped me. He said, "You're right. I can't bring your husband back. I can't bring your baby back. I can't give you a job—but I can help you to learn to live again."

And with the help of God, he did.

Summing Up

Discover the truths found in Psalm 121 and Isaiah 43:1-5 anew every day:

Shall I look to the mountain gods for help? No! My help is from Jehovah who made the mountains! And the heavens too! He will never let me stumble, slip or fall. For he is always watching, never sleeping.

Jehovah himself is caring for you! He is your defender. He protects you day and night. He keeps you from all evil, and preserves your life. He keeps his eye upon you as you come and go, and always guards you.

Psalm 121 TLB

Don't be afraid, for I have ransomed you; I have called you by name; you are mine.

When you go through deep waters and great trouble, I will be with you. When you go through rivers of difficulty, you will not drown! When you walk through the fire of oppression, you will not be burned up—the flames will not consume you.

For I am the LORD your God . . . you are precious to
me and honored, and I love you.

Isaiah 43:1-5 TLB

You may not believe it now, but some day the sun will
shine again—and brighter!
God planned it so.

Reflection

No Gain Without Pain

You reminded
me again, today,
Lord.
There is no gain
without pain.
I must be
making headway
because I hurt.
Hallelujah!
Amen.

ROBERT H. SCHULLER

Positive Prayers for Power-Filled Living (Bantam, 1985)

PART 3

Your Hope for Wholeness

You notice little changes in the way you're feeling and reacting. You're not so explosive anymore. You don't spend hours crying or raging. You have accepted the fact that life will go on, and you are beginning to make decisions that will bring you comfort.

But this new way of life is so foreign to you that you almost miss the days of rage and anger!

Questions plague you:

Will you ever be whole again?
Will you ever be joyful again?
Will you ever feel the presence of God again?

Yes! But you may not recognize the signs of growth, for they are often as strange as the grief itself.

God has a special plan for your divorce recovery. Reading this book may be a part of his healing process in your life, but he will not give you exactly what he gave me. He loves you and values your uniqueness too much to give you something he made for another. When your readiness matches his timing, he will lead you into wholeness. Search for it—through friends, through ministers, through social gatherings, through counselors, through service, through Bible study, through reading, through prayer. But do not let others make you feel guilty because you do not have what they have. Instead, seek God's plan, tailored especially—and only—for you!

Pray, as you read this section, that God will use it to speak to you and that he will guide you into wholeness. I will be sharing from my experience and from the collective experience of others who have shared their grief with me. I will point out some danger signs—times when I thought I was whole, but I had really only built a scab over my wound. Pray that God will show you areas in your life where you, too, have formed a scab; but you need to heal and grow. I will be sharing from the secret places of my heart, and writing in this manner makes me feel vulnerable. Please pray for me as you read, for I find my survival as a writer dependent on the prayers of my friends. And pray that God will give you the courage, insight, and strength to pay the price to be fully whole.

Wholeness will not be an easy journey. My friends, in discussing this issue, remind me that I *am* growing if I have asked God to help me grow, even when I cannot see I am making progress. It is a steep, sometimes discouraging climb; but oh, how beautiful the mountaintop!

Reflection

As I looked back over my life I realized that until the divorce my public "identity" had been pretty clear and well defined. I had been first a son, then a husband, a father, a businessman-turned-writer and a Christian speaker. But now I realized that these identification marks all had to do with *what I did,* not *who I was.*

—when a person "comes out" and is honest about who he or she really is—with true feelings attached—and is sort of emotionally naked before us on any significant level, I have found him or her always to have a haunting family resemblance to Jesus Christ.

KEITH MILLER, ANDREA WELLS MILLER

The Single Experience (Word, 1981)

28

Those Ever-changing Emotions

In the very early stages of grief, you know you have made progress when you admit your anger and move away from feelings of numbness, humiliation, rejection, longing, and hurt. So the next change is a strange one: *you know you're getting better when you're numb instead of angry.* You have worked through your anger. It probably happened in stages. You thought you had it under control; then, in an unsuspecting moment, it would erupt again. The process was exhausting. Now, perhaps, you're just tired of the strife and want peace. You don't question the fact that life is unfair, and you don't react to tragedy or triumph. You just exist.

You no longer need to lash out at your former husband. You actually pray (sometimes) that God will save him rather than destroy him.

You don't get upset (often) over little things that used to bring on a pity party, an angry rage, or a bout of belittling yourself.

You accept the good and the bad of life as normal and don't often even bother to respond to it.

You no longer think you caused whatever trouble happens around you. You realize that it is simply a part of life.

You don't get excited over much of anything, and you don't get upset over much of anything.

Yes, as strange as it may seem, this is a sign of growth. *You're getting better.*

But beware! You're not whole yet. This change simply shows you have stopped bleeding and begun to heal. You now have a scab over your divorce wound. You have moved from the stage of anger to the stage of depression. Much growth must take place before you are ready for a new relationship and/or for God's great, bright, tailored-especially-for-you tomorrow.

When you hear yourself having a version of the following conversations, move cautiously! These are signs of impending danger at this stage in your recovery. They are tools the enemy uses to keep you from life victorious.

"It's time I got my life together now. The fellow I've been dating is such a nice person. Maybe I should marry him. They tell me our love will grow."

or:

"The children need a father, and he's really a good person."

or:

"It's silly of me to be wasting all this time alone. I should find some good person and settle down."

Remember that no one deserves to be married to someone who does not truly love him or her—and you don't really want to spend your life with someone who happened along when you were lonely (unless that someone, in your eyes, also happens to be the greatest person God ever created).

I almost fell into this trap. I dated some very fine men who would have made good fathers for my child and good husbands—but not mine, at that time in my life. Well-meaning people, who truly cared about me and wished me happiness, would tell me that I wouldn't love the same way the second time around. As I struggled with this thought, I finally vowed that I would never marry again unless I felt I was the luckiest person in the world. The man I marry deserves that kind of love and devotion from me, and I deserve that kind of love and devotion from him.

Becoming a person who can develop an intimate relationship—the kind God delights to give us—requires growth time in addition to healing time. A good marriage does not grow from soil called I'm-no-longer-angry- and-it's-time-I-got-my-life-together.

Reflection

My family prayed for years that God would send a wonderful man into my life to heal my broken heart. (I did, too!) The day finally came when we realized we had been praying for the wrong thing. We needed to

pray that God would heal my broken heart and make
me a whole person, so I would be ready for whatever
form of happiness he chose to send me.

> Delight yourself in the LORD, and He will
> give you the desires of your heart.
>   Psalm 37:4 (NAS)

29

The Ugly Word

You know you're getting better when you can say the word *divorced*. It doesn't come easily, and you may go through an entire grief cycle over just that one word.

First, you go through denial:

This can't be happening to me!
I'll wake up tomorrow and everything will be okay.
It's a phase he's going through.
I'll claim God's promises and praise him, and a miracle will happen, and this will go away.

(*Do* claim God's promises, praise him, and pray for a miracle. *Don't* move on until he frees you to do so. But remember: denial is early in your divorce grief. Once God has released you *or* your former spouse has remarried, you must leave behind you thoughts of reconciliation and think, instead, of rebuilding. In God's

time, if his miracle of reconciliation is rejected by
your loved one, he will free you to move on.)

Now comes the gamut of emotions:

You're embarrassed every time you have to check
DIVORCED when you fill out a form.
Then you're angry that they would even ask you to
check DIVORCED. It is none of "their" business.
You say harsh words to people who make unknow-
ing, unkind remarks; and you get a warped satisfaction from bragging to others about how you
"put her in her place."

And you bargain:

Perhaps a legal separation is in order. Then you
won't have that "stigma."
You ask God to send someone new into your life
quickly, knowing that when remarriage takes
place you will no longer have to tell anyone
you're divorced.
You make promises to God—and to your spouse.

Depression sets in, usually in the form of self-pity:

"Nobody else has been in my situation, and no one
cares or understands."
"Others deserve to be divorced, but not me!"
"She doesn't have *anything* to offer. So why does she
have *my* husband?"
"What's wrong with me?"
"I can't go on."

Finally, a gracious God brings acceptance and healing:

> "This is me. I'm divorced. I never thought it would ever happen to me, but it has. And I, God's child, am an okay person in spite of my divorce. I don't like it. I didn't want it. I don't believe in divorce. But I know that God loves me and accepts me as I am. I can accept myself, too, and move on."

It took me an entire year, but I finally got that awful word out of my mouth. Someone asked me, and I said the words *I'm divorced.* The words hurt, and I cringed even as I said them; but I realized the fact that they had finally found their way out of *my* mouth was a major accomplishment.

A few weeks later, I ran into a college friend I hadn't seen recently. She asked the fatal question: "Where is he?" And I said quickly, "We're separated." I cringed, even as the words were spoken. But I couldn't bring myself to correct them and tell her the truth. I was back in denial again. It just happened! I couldn't say *the word.*

Five years later, I received comments from the editor regarding the Epilogue to *Justin, Heaven's Baby.* Highly complimentary, it said, "We need to make only one major change. You never, ever said you were divorced; it needs to be said."

There it was again! That ugly word! And there *I* was, *five years later,* back in denial. But this time I had grown. It didn't stab me the way it did at first. In fact, I had a good laugh over it. I understood grief so I realized that this backsliding was normal. And I knew who I was and whose I was. As God's children, we are first-class citizens, regardless of where he found us.

I still don't like the word. I still don't think divorce should happen in Christian homes. I still have trouble really accepting the fact that it happened to me— but it did. Yet I am whole because I serve a great God who is able, out of the shambles of my life, to bring harmony and peace and beauty and wholeness and rebirth.

Reflection

To abide under the "shadow of the Almighty" is to live free from fear of irredeemable circumstances! Although problems, frustrations, tragedies enter our lives, we know that not one of them is beyond "working together for good" OR "shadow of the Almighty" would have deterred it.

So . . . we can know that on whatever "ground" we find ourselves, He will be with us . . . and, if we allow, He will ultimately, in His time, in His way, redeem every tear, every anguish, every sorrow.

When Christ dwells in me, then the ground on which I stand is holy ground because He is standing on it too. And because He is a Redeemer God, He will enable me to make creative use of all, even unpleasant circumstances.

RUTH VAUGHN

My God! My God! (Impact)

30

Mellowing

Y ou know you're getting better when you move in from your life's extremes.

You may have reacted by running—from one party to another; from one friend to another; from one relationship to another; shopping; losing yourself in sports or hobbies. Whatever it is, it keeps you from having to think or feel. You come home late and exhausted with barely enough energy left to kiss your children good night before you, too, collapse in bed.

You're getting better when you can (at least now and then) actually enjoy a quiet evening at home.

You may have reacted by hiding. You withdrew from life. You stayed home a lot and watched a lot of television. Television, too, can keep you from thinking or feeling. And you sleep a lot. You just don't know where your energy has gone, but about the time you tuck in the children, you, too, begin to yawn. You sleep for hours longer than you should and have trouble getting out of bed in the morning. You hide in a corner at parties (to which you go only when forced).

You're getting better when spending another evening at home alone is more threatening than venturing out. You may brave up enough to go to a Singles Retreat or to call a friend and ask him/her to join you for dinner. You don't do this every week or every night at first, but the feeling that you need people is the first sign that you are getting better.

You may have reacted by rejecting that which was a positive part of your life when you were married. Often it is church. Church people try, but they don't really know how to treat divorce within. Divorce is not God's ideal, and they are afraid of condoning it, so they overreact and, subconsciously, reject the person rather than the sin. Too often they take the side of the one who remains rather than reaching out with God's love to both parties; and rarely do they reach out in such circumstances when a person doesn't come to them first. This is wrong; and piled on top of the loss of your mate is the loss of former friendships and fellowship as you once knew it. Your hurt and bitterness toward church people and your mutual friends may drive you away. You may, for a while, even feel betrayed by God.

You're getting better when you sense your need for God. You're getting better, again, when you forgive his people (who, incidentally, are completely unaware that they wronged you) and take those first—and awkward—steps back to find fellowship. A Christian singles group, retreat, or ski trip is a good place to begin.

It seems that most people become their opposite when going through grief. The person who entertained a lot and enjoyed social activities suddenly becomes a recluse. The person who was outgoing may actually appear shy. The person who enjoyed quiet time alone may become a socialite.

You're getting better when the "real you" begins, again, to emerge. And the *real you* is now tempered with your opposite, making you a more balanced person. You see, God brings growth even when you don't know it's happening!

Reflection

She said, "When they introduced you to speak, I thought, 'Wow! God must have done something wonderful for her. She's the one who hides in the corner all the time.'"

You did, Lord. You returned me to my natural self. Out of the shambles of my life, you grew joy and hope.

I thought my real life had ended and I was just existing until I got to heaven. But not you! You never, ever quit seeing me as the person you were helping me become.

Thank you, Lord. In spite of me, you never gave up.

31

The New You

You're getting better when you learn whose you are and who you are.

If you have given your life to God, you are his child.

> And if children, then heirs; heirs of God, and joint-heirs with Christ; if so be that we suffer with him, that we may be also glorified together.
>
> Romans 8:17

If you are God's child, he shares in your suffering; and, as you face your life's disappointments holding his hands, you share in his. Knowing that you have him, you can begin to learn who you are—for you have had a crisis-identity change. As you travel with him, you find your new identity, a little at a time.

Seeking your new identity:

You no longer tolerate long periods of negative self-talk.

You accept your many roles in life: single parent, divorcee, friend, employee, breadwinner, head of the household, and on and on!

You put your home in order (at least a million times if you, like me, belong to the "order of messies"!).

You quit trying to be that which you can never be—like a father to your children.

You admit to God and others your need for help, and you try to allow your children friendships with Christian men who can become positive role models to them, filling some of the void.

You share your heavenly Father's love with your children, for ultimately his love is what will bring them—and you—wholeness.

You find a sense of self-esteem in your work. Finding this sense of self-esteem may mean months or years of schooling (sometimes one class at a time) to train for the career you gave up in exchange for marriage. It may mean a new commitment to integrity in the way you fulfill your obligations at work. It may mean accepting, in your heart, the fact that you must work now even though you have always believed that mothers should stay at home. Whatever your dilemma, God understands and shares those feelings and desires with you. He will help you on your journey.

But these changes don't happen all at once. They seem to come in waves of acceptance followed by undertows of denial. It took me a long time to accept the fact that I could not replace a father in my son's life. I agonized over this fact for *years* before I finally gave it to the Lord and asked him to supply what I could not.

It was no coincidence that, after my release, God opened my eyes to see what he was already doing for my son. Several older teens and Christian men played special roles in his life. None replaced his missing father, but God revealed to me that he was tailoring my son's wholeness, just as he was tailoring mine!

Grief, anger, and bitterness blind us to God's handiwork—and sometimes postpone or prevent his work in our lives and in the lives of those we love. As you struggle to know your new identity, ask God to open your eyes to see what he is already doing for you.

Reflection

We look at ourselves—

Assess our strengths,
Cringe at our weaknesses,
Construct a box
And crawl inside.

We tell God to make a difference . . .

As long as we get to stay
    inside the box.

GLAPHRE

When the Pieces Don't Fit . . . (Zondervan, 1984)

32

Forgiven . . . I Repeat It! I'm Forgiven

Perhaps the most beautiful part of your growth comes when you truly accept God's forgiveness and forgive yourself. Even you who were victims and didn't choose your divorce may struggle with this, and many a thoughtless remark will send you into another unhealthy bout of soul searching.

Sometimes we *are* guilty. God's gift of forgiveness through salvation is freely available to us—all we have to do is ask.

Sometimes we carry guilt for situations and/or sins we have caused or committed. Although God has forgiven us, we have trouble forgiving ourselves.

Sometimes our guilt is not valid but it tortures us. We have asked God to forgive us; but we continue, in our minds, to replay scenes from our marriage where we acted immaturely. We judge ourselves harshly for every mistake we made. This is a common tool the enemy uses to defeat us.

Whether our guilt is real or imagined, God has given us promises:

> If we confess our sins, he is faithful and just to forgive us our sins, *and to cleanse us from all unrighteousness.*
>
>   1 John 1:9 (italics added)

> As far as the east is from the west, so far hath he removed our transgressions from us.
>
>   Psalm 103:12

> I, even I, am he that blotteth out thy transgressions for mine own sake, and *will not remember thy sins.*
>   Isaiah 43:25 (italics added)

Regardless of the validity of your guilt, hold his hand, ask forgiveness, forgive yourself, and move on. *We do not have the right to hold a grudge against one whom God has forgiven.* Sometimes we are that one who stands forgiven. We err if we do not also forgive ourselves.

If our guilt is invalid and/or if we can't seem to forgive ourselves and move on, we need to seek professional help. Begin with your minister; then seek a Christian counselor to help you. Keep seeking help until you find it.

Reflection

I said, "If you knew, you wouldn't want me;
My scars are hidden by the face I wear."

He said, "My child, my scars go deeper;
It was love for you that put them there."

Forgiven, I repeat it, I'm forgiven;
Clean before my Lord I freely stand.

Forgiven, I can dare forgive my brother;
Forgiven, I reach out to take your hand.

WILLIAM J. AND GLORIA GAITHER

33

You Serve Again

You know you're getting better when you realize that you can serve God alone. Grief is a very selfish thing. You are so obsessed by your situation that you feel useless—especially if you served God in some special way as a couple, you feel impotent alone.

Sometimes God jars us out of our self-pity in dramatic ways. Sometimes he lets us move forward, slowly, on our own.

Sometimes we withdraw from areas of responsibility. Other times we bury ourselves in service to others or continue our lives' routines, but our hearts aren't in it, and we don't "feel" good about it. We may even feel hypocritical for serving when our lives aren't perfect.

One sign of wholeness is when, finally, we realize we have been empowered by the Holy Spirit in an area of service to him. Usually, with this realization come tears of gratitude and a tenderness we thought had gone forever.

One way we serve again is by praying for others. While in the midst of my divorce grief, on the heels of burying my infant son, my sister had a premature baby, hospitalized with complications. I was miles from her, agonizing alone in my big, empty home-turned-house. One day I was especially distraught in a futile effort to pray for them, and I cried in angry agony to God, "Where are you, God? What's going on here? Why am I in more turmoil for her than I was when my own son was dying? What happened to your peace and your power, and where is it in my life now?"

God didn't speak audibly, but his message was clear: "She prayed so I could send you peace. Now it's your turn."

I can't tell you I felt any better about my situation, and I can't tell you I felt my prayers were heard. But I can assure you that I prayed, for I knew what it was like to receive peace and power through the prayers of those who love me.

This was the first of many times God had to move me dramatically away from my propensity toward self-pity. When you begin to carry a burden for another, you are on your way to building your own wholeness.

Reflection

He who doesn't really believe "It is more blessed to give than to receive" . . .

has never needed.

34

The Sexual, Single You

You know you're getting better when you come to terms with both your sexuality and your Christianity. You realize that you are powerless alone to withstand sexual temptation. You give your sexuality to God, admitting your frustration, potential lack of control, and obsession. You ask—maybe even demand—that he handle it for you.

You may go through a period of time when you are sexually nonfeeling—you have absolutely no desire. You are afraid that you will never experience desire *or* fulfillment again—in fact, sometimes this fear tortures you. Coupled with the fear of never having fulfillment is the fear that you will be unable to respond to another—*ever*—even should you someday remarry.

Fortunately—and unfortunately—these periods of numbness do not last long. When this numbness leaves you, it leaves suddenly and catches you off guard, burning with passion.

You may go through periods of time when your sexuality is expressed through your unconscious, through dreams and fantasies. These come without warning and usually leave you awake in the middle of the night, frustrated and angry.

When you finally begin to date, you discover that your body has forgotten that a good-night kiss should mean an end to your evening rather than a beginning. The married you has learned to enjoy your body's response to the embrace and closeness of another. You may be shocked to discover that your body can—and will—continue to respond even when no thoughts of love are involved. Adding to this dilemma is the fact that you don't want your body to quit responding. Frustrating as this stage may seem, it is better than the numbness and fear that possessed you for a while. Jim Smoke, in his book *Growing Through Divorce,* titles a chapter "Thirty-Seven, Going on Seventeen." Imagining seventeen-year-old passion in a thirty-seven-year-old body, well experienced in sexual response, gives you a glimpse of the dilemma you face as a single again.

You go through periods of being angry at God for creating you a sexual being, and arguing with him about whether or not you should control your passion. You may even search the Scriptures and have long discussions on law and grace, trying to justify postmarital sex biblically. Many singles never move beyond this fight with God.

You may go through periods of time when you are obsessed with your sexuality. Your sexual dilemma occupies your every waking moment and robs your thoughts of their former creativity.

You may try all those things you used to tell your teenagers would work—cold showers, physical exercise, getting involved in some creative project. These, however, work only while you're taking the shower or playing the game of volleyball or jogging or sewing. The moment you stop, passion returns—often stronger.

You are on your way to wholeness when you realize that another's comments do not make you wrong for having sexual feelings—and that you do not have to change her/his mind. Many times a well-meaning married person will comment that a lack of sex in your life should not be an issue. Often they will pass on "wise words" such as the fact that you need not feel sorry for yourself—they don't indulge every night either. It took me a long time to accept the fact that the married would never understand the sexual dilemma of the formerly married! Now I entitle them to their opinions; and rarely, anymore, do I feel compelled to help them understand what it's like *never* to be fulfilled and to even rarely experience a loving embrace. Sometimes I can even find it in my heart to pray that God will bless their marriage and give them a long, fulfilled life so they will never have to understand what I tried so futilely to share.

You are on your way to living with your sexuality when you face God with it—in honesty, in submission, without anger. The God who created you a sexual being fully understands your dilemma and knows how to deal with it. He alone can deliver you from your frustrations, but he doesn't do it without your permission.

Each of us will have a separate key to finding peace in the arena of our sexuality. For me, it was confessing to God that I had been rebellious and angry with him. I had lived by his rules when I married the first time, and I was angry that he hadn't rewarded me with a lifelong marriage. Once I told him I would serve him all my life, whether or not I was happily married and sexually fulfilled; once I asked his forgiveness for my rebellion; once I gave him my obsession with my sexuality and asked him to control it for me or free me from the turmoil of desire laced with guilt—I was free.

Yes, I am still a sexual being, and there are still times when I feel sexually frustrated; but I am no longer obsessed with my sexuality.

Reflection

A Silent Hunger

My love must wait. Still, there's an appetite
That drives me to the tasting of that fruit
That never should be picked so green. The night
Stirs my desire and summons up a brute
That's always ravenous when he awakes.
No logic quiets him. No piety
Can make the bruin rest. His fire forsakes
All love and feeds on frothing chemistry.
How well you wait; avoid the hurried slur
Of love that can't forgo her meal one day.
Temperance alone waits best—prefers
The total soul, thus orders need away.
When love contrives the whole, then love is good.
And hurried need reduces love to food.

CALVIN MILLER

If This Be Love (Harper & Row, 1985)

35

Responsibility

Y ou know you're getting better when you accept responsibility for your life.

You quit looking for reasons to call him and struggle to resolve your life's situations without his help. You used to create problems so he would know you needed him—and, secretly—so he would have to give up a little of his freedom to help you.

You quit blaming him and your divorce for everything you want to do that is questionable and for everything you should do, but don't.

You quit accepting tiredness or listlessness as normal and seek to change how you feel. This may mean seeking medical help or counseling. It may mean improving your diet—reducing junk food or sweets. It may mean developing an exercise program. More than likely, it will mean ALL OF THE ABOVE!

You go back to school or find a job, striving for financial independence. You honestly endeavor to live within your budget. You seek financial assistance if you need it; you seek to free yourself from financial assistance if the time is right for you to assume this responsibility for yourself and your children.

You buy things for yourself without feeling guilty *and* without overspending. In most areas of your life now, there is a veil preventing your eyes from seeing beauty. In the early stages of your divorce, clothes are made only in colors that don't look good on you or with price tags you can't afford. As you get better, so does your selection of clothes.

You ask God's forgiveness for the attitudes that keep you from being productive. This may be resentment toward someone who has a happy marriage. It may be bitterness that your ex is financially independent, but you struggle to place a decent meal on your table. This may be anger toward a church and church friends who judged you unfairly. And the list goes on. Whatever it is that eats away inside you, preventing you from abundant living, can be given to God in an act of confession. Only when you are free from the burden of hate will you have enough energy to live for today.

Reflection

So the judge gave me custody of Jason Towner—200-plus pounds. I recall thinking, "I'll never sur-

vive." So many things I had taken for granted . . . I
didn't even know how to operate the washer and dryer
that were now mine. I had always conned Jane into
doing all the mundane things I did not want to do. . . .
Like a lot of husbands, I had this way of doing things
only half right until Jane would finally say in exas-
peration, "Oh, here, let me do it."

> Now, if Jason gained weight,
>   Jason was responsible.
> If Jason needed laundry done,
>   Jason was responsible.
> If Jason needed money,
>   Jason was responsible.

JASON TOWNER

Jason Loves Jane (but they got a Divorce) (Impact, 1978).
Used by permission of Zondervan Publishing House.

36

Forgive Him?
Surely You Jest!

Forgiveness comes in two stages, and you may need to deal with both to become completely whole. To motivate you to pay this price, remember that you're not ready for remarriage until your former marriage is no longer consuming a part of your today.

The first stage of forgiveness takes place in your heart. You forgive him—*truly forgive.* You no longer need revenge. It is impossible to truly forgive one who has wronged you without the healing touch of God. The task is not easy. You may have come to God many times saying, "I'm tired of hurting this way. Help me to forgive and heal." And for some reason it doesn't happen. Friends might tell you that you were not truly repentant, but that is of little help as you struggle between "what ought" and "what is."

Some suggestions: first, be as honest with God as you can be. Your prayer might start out something like:

"God, I know you want me to forgive. But I'm really enjoying hating him right now. Help me." Or, another day, it may sound more like:

"God, he doesn't deserve my forgiveness!"

You move beyond that point, if for no other reason, because hatred hurts you rather than him. Later prayers might sound like:

"Father, I don't like feeling this way, but I don't know how to change. He really wronged me, and he doesn't deserve my forgiveness—but I want to heal. Please change me." Then, as you work out, give of yourself, or write out your anger (using the strategies from Part 2 and those you invent on your own), be sure to ask God to do his part. You may not feel God at work, answering your prayer; but if you have asked him to, he has begun to prepare you for the work of forgiveness.

What happens when time has passed, and you have tried, but that welling resentment remains? Keep giving it to God as you become aware of it. Most of my friends tell me their release was sudden—and that it took much longer than they thought it would. Sometimes they were aware of God taking it during prayer or praise; other times, they awoke one morning to realize they weren't bitter anymore—and then thanked God. This is God's healing, and people tell me it happens when "our readiness matches his timing." That is different for each of us.

If God healed your anger and bitterness instantaneously, without your having to spend months or years in the process, be sure to praise him! That is a rare gift. Most people have to struggle to be free.

The next stage of forgiveness takes place by mouth or by pen. You communicate your forgiveness to him and/or ask his forgiveness.

You may be irate that I would suggest this. You may be thinking, *Well, that's easy for her to say, but my divorce was not my fault. I don't have anything to ask forgiveness for.*

I didn't either. I, too, was the victim. I, too, heard speakers and read books and thought, *They just don't understand my situation—mine is different from all other divorces.* But I, too, when I had allowed God to work within me and when enough time had passed (*seven years* for me because of my compounded grief and stubbornness), heard his voice saying:

"Your sins toward him were intended to keep him or to bring him back. But there were times when you did not treat him with dignity, and there were many times you tried to manipulate him into doing things your way. And even though there were many more times when he did not treat you with respect, you weren't justified in mistreating him."

Writing my letter of apology took place seven years after our initial separation. Even then, it was not an easy letter to write. It was never acknowledged; I don't know whether he has accepted my forgiveness or not. But God doesn't ask us to secure forgiveness— just to ask for it. God doesn't ask us to wait for them to request our forgiveness—just to forgive. We are responsible for our actions, not their responses.

A word of caution is in order. *Don't fake it!* Don't ask forgiveness until you can't live another minute with-

out it. Otherwise this, too, becomes an act of manip-
ulation—one done in Jesus' name.

Some of you may feel frustrated because God is
dealing with you in this area, but your ex is deceased
or you don't know how to get in contact with him. In
these instances, you can write a letter and offer that
letter to God in an act of prayer, asking him to become
your messenger.

Wholeness will come when you acknowledge your
part in the failure of your marriage—however unin-
tentional it may have been—and allow God to trans-
form you so you don't end up in the same situation
again (our past has a strange way of repeating itself).

This may be especially difficult for those of you who
were victims in your divorce. Some of you weren't told
there were problems in your marriage—you just
awoke one day to find it had ended. Others of you
carried the load of guilt—or blame—for every problem you faced. In these instances, I suggest praying
with David, "Search me, O God, and know my heart;
try me, and know my thoughts." (Ps. 139:23). Ask
God to give you wisdom and to lead you into wholeness. His route to wholeness may be that of professional help, and seeking his wisdom will open that
door. Whatever channel he uses to help you, you will
find him faithful.

For most people, the issue of forgiveness is their
final act of healing. Sometimes it comes long after the
rest of the issues surrounding the divorce have been
resolved.

Reflection

How do we dispose of our need for revenge? By forgiving those who hurt us. THERE IS NO OTHER WAY! And what does it mean to forgive? Simply this: *Forgiving is surrendering your right to hurt back.*

. . . As we willingly give up our need to hurt back, we heal our memory of its power to hurt us.

. . . Since forgiveness is designed to protect us from our own anger, it is not necessary for our enemies to admit their guilt or ask forgiveness.

ARCHIBALD D. HART

Children and Divorce (Word, 1985)

37

Little Rays of Sunshine

You find yourself riding a ski lift for the tenth time, and you glance behind you and gasp at the beauty of God's creation. Then you realize that you have spent an entire weekend just flowing with the crowd, not really feeling anything, and completely oblivious to the beauty that surrounds you. At first, you are so overwhelmed by emotions of gratitude that you cringe from them. Then you are overcome with emotion as you realize that God's touch has found you—you thought it had gone forever.

Sometimes these glimpses send tears to your eyes. Sometimes they are such a contrast to your soul's darkness that you can only glance and must quickly look away. Nevertheless, seeing God's creation with your heart is his sign that your sun will shine again—in his time. It is his gift to you—your personal rainbow!

These things happen in phases. When you're hurting, you can handle only a little bit of God's love at a

108

time; and when you first experience beauty and joy, you may withdraw. As was mentioned earlier, it is not uncommon, during early grief, to develop migraine headaches that prevent you from participating in the social activity you had planned. Nor is it uncommon, when you force yourself to go, for you to develop hives or other physical ailments. You see, your self-esteem has been shattered and although you may find it hard to admit, you do not think you are worthy of so-called fun. But the glimpses of God's love come again and again, and you find yourself able to respond a little more each time.

You've moved a little further toward wholeness when you find yourself able to respond to God's Word, God's touch, and God's goodness. As my soul midnight ended and I began to rebuild, I found myself feeling like a dry sponge—I just couldn't get enough of God. Prior to that, I sought him in frustration and found him silent. Then he sought me—as on the ski lift—but I was too depressed to respond. When this hide-and-seek begins to end and you give yourself permission to enjoy life and God's creation again, you have moved another step toward wholeness.

Reflection

As I look back, Lord, I can see your hand in so many ways, but few that I recognized at the time. Money was always a problem so I didn't play much. When I signed up for a weekend retreat or planned a vacation, I would usually cancel at the last minute for lack of funds. Money didn't come when I thought I needed

it most. It came occasionally, though, as an affirmation, like the day I had decided to cancel the ski trip
because I couldn't afford it.

My hindsight tells me that was your way to saying,
"It's okay to have fun. Go. You're worth it!" I didn't
know that then. I spent so much fun-time in numbness: "Are we having fun yet?"

But you kept showing me the sunrise.

38

Fears, Obsessions, Bitternesses

Fear is often one of the first insurmountable obstacles women alone encounter. When you face your fears and work through them, you emerge stronger and begin your journey to wholeness.

Our fears are sometimes so irrational. We are afraid of going out, and we are afraid of staying home. We are afraid of loving, and we are afraid of never loving again. We are afraid of living alone, but we are afraid to share our home with another. We are afraid of being dependent, but we are afraid of becoming independent.

For me, the key to conquering fear was confession. Once I recognized that a large part of the agony I felt was fear, I spilled it out in prayer. Knowing that "perfect love casteth out fear" only pointed out my inadequacies. The God of compassion didn't lead me to that Scripture and tell me to love him more. He led me, instead, to a Scripture that assured me he was bigger than my problem. He led me to "Jehovah who made the mountains," found in *The Living Bible,* Psalm 121. Through this Scripture, he brought me peace. This deliverance from neurotic fear, for me, was instantaneous and complete. It was, however, the *only* part of my entire divorce struggle from which I experienced deliverance.

Obsessions are quite different. They rob us of our energy and creativity by consuming our every waking moment and overpowering our every thought. We may be obsessed by our loneliness, our fear, our lack of financial independence, our sexuality, our failure. We may play out our obsessions in a number of ways, including negative self-talk, fantasizing, and ceaseless talking.

Once we release our obsessions into the hands of God, he can free us again to live. Releasing them, though, is not easy and usually comes in stages. In the early stages, we may need to displace our obsession. For example, we may play an aggressive game of volleyball or golf, talking to God as we hit the ball about the lack of sex in our lives and our anger and frustration over it. Then we may use our creative energies to write a letter or a song about our obsession with loneliness. Perhaps it was someone recovering from a divorce who penned the words to the song "I'm so lonely I could die." And, instead, we may be so obsessed with our failure in marriage that we teach a Sunday school lesson on success. These are all creative, positive ways to deal with obsessions in our lives.

Ultimately, confessing our obsession to God; admitting we are powerless without his help; and asking him to free us is what brings release. This, however, is not as simple as it appears in writing, for our entire being must be ready before it is possible for us to pray that prayer. Use creative ways to deal with your obsessions until the right time comes for giving it to God.

Releasing our *bitterness* is a more conscious choice. Bitterness is associated with anger and rage about our situation. Along with the anger is denial. Usually others tell us we need to get over our bitterness, and we tell them we don't have any such thing. In fact, it makes us mad that they think we do. Then we admit to bitterness, but we feel quite self-righteous about having it. After all, anyone in our situation would have the right to be bitter! We usually enjoy being bitter for a while before we realize that bitterness can destroy us.

I do not believe we can release our bitterness by simply deciding to. Instead, we give it to God and let him heal us. And since God doesn't fit well into our preconceived boxes, he delivers us in a multitude of ways. Some he delivers instantaneously; some must work out their deliverance; some heal gradually; and some of us need professional help to be free.

When we have truly recovered from our divorce, we have experienced the healing touch of God. You notice that in final analysis, the key to resolving fears, obsessions, and bitternesses is our admission and release for God's healing touch. If you are in the early stages of grief, this will sound pious and trite. Reading it may even make you angry. First, you must survive your trauma, using the keys found in Part 2. But once you survive, healing and growth are conscious choices.

Without faith, I don't believe it is possible for us to suffer the trauma of a broken home and emerge whole. Healthy, alive, whole singles are always testimony to the fact of God's healing touch.

Reflection

I like storybook endings. I'd like to tell you that, after that experience, God put the pieces of my life together, and we all lived happily ever after. I'd like to say that loneliness disappeared and that, though all of us were changed, life was better. I can't quite come to that place, but I do know that with God's love and mercy I can live my life as I must, without the demon fear robbing me.

39

The Sweet Voice
of God's Love

You know you're getting better when you sense God's presence in your life. As you near the end of your period of numbness, you will experience times when God touches you and you are overwhelmed. Often you respond with tears of joy and realize how strange they feel and how long it has been since you trusted your emotions enough to let them respond to God. For some reason, God seems silent a lot in the early stages of grief. When you begin to sense his presence more often, you know you are on your way to wholeness.

Sometimes you will hear a song and discover that God has spoken to you in its message. You may read a scripture that jumps off the page to touch your heart. You may see a rainbow and feel God's tender touch of affirmation. Tears may cloud your eyes, as you realize how long it has been since you did more than go through the motions of worship. This breakthrough is a sign that your morning is dawning, and you are nearing the end of your bondage.

Reflection

Meanwhile, where is God? This is one of the most disquieting symptoms. When you are happy, so happy that you have no sense of needing Him, so happy that you are tempted to feel His claims upon you as an interruption, if you remember yourself and turn to Him with gratitude and praise, you will be—or so it feels—welcomed with open arms. But go to Him when your need is desperate, when all other help is vain, and what do you find? A door slammed in your face, and a sound of bolting and double bolting on the inside. After that, silence. . . .

I have gradually been coming to feel that the door is no longer shut and bolted. Was it my own frantic need that slammed it in my face? The time when there is nothing at all in your soul except a cry for help may be just the time when God can't give it: you are like a drowning man who can't be helped because he clutches and grabs. Perhaps your own reiterated cries deafen you to the voice you hoped to hear.

C. S. LEWIS

A Grief Observed (Harper & Row, 1963)
Used by permission.

40

Giving God Permission

God is so careful of our feelings. He will never force us to use our sorrow; but when we give him permission, he will affirm us as he uses our testimony to help another. He never rushes us. With patience and tenderness, he lets us move out a little at a time.

Reflection

Well-meaning people would tell me,
"God will use this to help someone!"
I could see excitement in their eyes.

Forgive me, God, but I just couldn't share their
    elation.
Instead, I said (bitterly, I confess—but true!)
"How exciting! I've prayed all my life I could be
    someone's bad example."

But now you're using it. It's not that way!
I should have known that you—you who spoke the
    words
"Let him who is without sin. . . ."

I should have trusted you to use it right.
I should have known that you give dignity—you do
    not take it away.
I should have trusted you sooner with my sorrow.

What greater joy than I could help
Another when his journey meets a snare.
How unworthy for this honor I find me.

But in your great creation you have planned
That when another reaches out his hand
And I reach mine responding in your name,

We neither one will ever be the same.
For Jesus' blood transforms this sorrow mine
And others see his hope, not my disgrace.

Summing Up

Divorce feels like being chopped into pieces. We were one whole—one unit. Now we are two bleeding, scarred half-pieces. The wound isn't even neat like half an apple when it's cut. It's a gape here, and a deep stab mark there, and a mass of bruises in various places, and a rending in a dozen other places. They're all bleeding and hurting at the same time, and we don't have gauze enough to go around. We pray to die, but death won't come.

Sometimes the stabbing and rending takes place during marriage and the scar tissue forms before the actual separation happens. Divorce, in these instances, feels like relief—it is so superior to the stabbing process. (Scabs and scars are less deadly than slowly bleeding to death!)

Either way, we face a problem. Someone who has just healed still has scabs and scar tissue that need to heal or to be removed. One who has new skin where scabs once lived is still in the "half" stage and needs to grow to become "whole" again.

But we can't see ourselves. We feel so together because our half-person with scar tissue and scabs is so much better than our bleeding person, begging to die. Now we face the danger of rebounding or of remarriage for the wrong reasons.

I challenge you to *wait!* To pay the price of removing the scar tissue. To let God give you a new identity and wholeness. To pay the price of developing intimate, Christ-like relationships.

God wants you to live a fulfilled, happy life. God wants your marriage to be intimate. God wants marriage on earth to be the nearest thing to heaven that we experience—he is the bridegroom, and we are his bride. But for him to give it to you, you must pay the price of finding wholeness. I pray that you will.

Reflection

I must conquer my loneliness alone.

I must be happy with myself
or I have
nothing
to offer.

Two halves have
little choice
but to join;
and yes,
they do
make a
whole.

but two
wholes
when they coincide . . .

that is
beauty.

that is
love.

PETER McWILLIAMS

How to Survive the Loss of a Love (Simon & Schuster)

Epilogue

Family and friends ask what they can do to help, but even their question reminds you of your inner hopelessness. Often you cannot look them in the eyes; occasionally you cannot even respond to their questions because that old, now-familiar lump replaces your ability to speak. When the words come, just hearing them serves to defeat you, for you know of only two responses:

"I don't know."

or

"Nothing."

Sometimes, in their efforts to help without asking, your family and friends hurt you instead—so often they say or do the wrong things. Perhaps this is because of their own fears—could they be next? Or perhaps their efforts hurt because your wound is so raw that even a healing balm at first brings pain. Sometimes your friends stay away from you—they feel so inadequate, and their own emotions choke them every time they try to reach out to you.

How to help someone who is going through a divorce is, in itself, a future book, but a few suggestions are offered here. This Epilogue is for your friends— and for you. Next time they say, "What can I do?" use one of these responses. Or better yet, loan them this book. Reading it will help them understand to a small degree what you are facing. This chapter will give them ideas that will help, not hurt. You might even underline those that speak especially to your need— and you might consider adding your own words before loaning it out.

Immediately after your loss, you might say:

Pray for me; right now I can't pray for myself.

Listen to me. Listen, and don't judge, edit, or ridicule. I've got to talk. Even let me say things we both know aren't true, for as long as these destructive thoughts are inside me I can't heal. Pray that God will heal my mind and clarify my thinking, but don't rebuke me for thinking or feeling the way I do right now.

Don't take sides—not even mine. If you criticize, I must defend. If you defend, I must criticize. Just love me, and be an impartial listener.

Let me join in on couples and group functions— and allow me to talk to the men (I won't attempt to steal them). The isolation I feel in being cut off from friendships that just weeks ago were normal threatens to destroy me—and even our friendship if I feel rejected, misjudged, or distrusted by you, too.

Insist I get out of the house periodically. Don't just invite me—come by to pick me up. If I have a headache, take me anyway; don't let me bury myself completely in my grief.

Don't suggest I go to singles functions—unless I mention it first. Instead, occasionally ask a single to invite me. And remember, it will take time before I am ready to respond.

Don't matchmake. I need time to heal first; dating or remarriage too soon usually brings on another divorce.

Call me often, just for a few minutes. I live in the home of the never-ringing telephone, and silence reinforces my hopelessness.

Send me cards, notes, and letters. If they include money, send them anonymously.

Share things that helped you in down times, but remember they may not help me right now.

Remind me—every time we meet—that this will pass and that you have confidence in me.

Pick up my children occasionally to allow me time alone. Don't say, "Would you like for me to . . . ?" Say instead, "I'll be by this afternoon, or would tomorrow be better?"

Give me records, tapes, mottos, or books of encouragement written in a short, easy-to-read style.

Don't try to speak for God.

Help me survive on Sundays—they are as tough on me as holidays, but I often wear a fake smile because it's hard for me to tell you I'm hurting—again.

Encourage others to invest time and love in my children. They desperately need a Christian role model the same sex as their missing parent.

In three to six months, you might say:

Any or all of the above plus . . .

Give me time! I'm a little better, but I'm not whole yet.

Don't try to tell me I'm getting better unless you can give me concrete examples as to how. I've probably just buried my hurt because I know you're tired of listening.

Help me find affordable professional help if I'm noticeably depressed, if my life is still in disorder, if I'm planning to be reunited soon but there is no joint effort on the part of my former spouse, or if you see signs about me or my children that alarm you.

Suggest an exercise or self-improvement program for both of us because *you* need it and want my company, not because *I* need to get my life together. I do, but I can't handle facing my faults right now.

Ask me for help—I need to move away from self-pity and to feel needed. If the other parent has custody, ask me if I want to baby-sit—I just might.

In one or two years, you might say:

Give me books that explain the grief process, divorce, loss—and books that give hope for rebuilding my life—and books on how to raise children alone. I can *finally* read again.

Help me move our relationship into a mutual friendship. For so long, it has been one-sided. Ask me for help—I so need to be needed and to give back of what I have received. I need to be a friend now, not just to have one.

Remember me on holidays, birthdays, Sundays, and occasional weekends—I'm better, but I still have down times when I don't think I'll survive.

Introduce me to a fine Christian man—with my permission, of course; I'm ready to reach out. Don't push me into serious dating, but give me the opportunity to develop my social skills again.

Ⅰt is so hard to allow people to help you—you feel so like a burden to the world. Let me assure you you're not. Your friends and family love you and want to see you happy, healthy, whole—even though it doesn't seem that way to you now. They will be grateful to you for telling them what you need. Besides, this is a good investment for them. You can never give them back what they have given you, but God keeps a scorecard. They have invested in you; and as you give of what you have received to others, they will reap a part of it as their eternal reward.

> . . . Come, you who are blessed of My Father, inherit the kingdom prepared for you from the foundation of the world.
> For I was hungry, and you gave Me something to eat; I was thirsty, and you gave Me drink . . . naked, and

you clothed Me; I was sick, and you visited Me . . .
. . . to the extent that you did it to one of these broth-
ers of Mine, even the least of them, you did it to Me.

Matthew 25:34-36; 40 (NAS)